# Octopus Mind

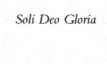

*Soli Deo Gloria*

# Octopus Mind

*Rachel Carney*

Seren is the book imprint of
Poetry Wales Press Ltd.
Suite 6, 4 Derwen Road, Bridgend, Wales, CF31 1LH
www.serenbooks.com
facebook.com/SerenBooks
twitter@SerenBooks

The right of Rachel Carney to be identified as
the author of this work has been asserted in accordance
with the Copyright, Designs and Patents Act, 1988.

ISBN: 9781781727102
Ebook: 9781781727119
A CIP record for this title is available from the British Library.

The publisher acknowledges the financial assistance of the Books Council of Wales.

Cover artwork: 'Noor' by Jason deCaires Taylor, 2021, Marine cement, 3m depth,
Eco Musée de Cannes

# Contents

# Apologies
*after Marcus Jackson*

Pardon my curtains.
They are no longer speaking to each other,
but I can't remember why.

I have left them open to the night –
staring at streetlights
and silence.

Pardon my circus.
It is drooping in the centre,
unwatched and unapplauded.

Pardon my mountain.
It is feeling
a little low today.

Pardon my starlings.
They are hungry, flighty
in the branches.

Pardon my muddy trainers.
One of them did not quite make it
to the shoe rack yesterday.

Pardon the piles of unread magazines,
the lack of trains in my station,
the confusion.

Pardon the waste food bin,
its stench emanating
from the kitchen floor.

Pardon the holes that appear when I'm not thinking,
the absentminded acrobats,
the grey tinge in the carpet.

Pardon the slow, wistful singing,
the sudden accident,
the yawning daffodils.

Pardon the missing persons,
the slip of waiting.
Pardon the universe you do not know.

# Octopus Self

It took me years
to tame the octopus of me,
to lure her out,

to show her that the world is safer than she thinks it is.

I set her high up on a rock,
where her colours merge and multiply.

Some days she basks in the shallows, content
with the strange shape of herself,

coiling, uncoiling,        confident, serene.

Or she swims out into deep ocean currents,
strong in her certainty, calm in her convictions.

Other days she cowers in the fissure of her lair,
sure that every shadow is a shark,
curled up around the bubble of her failure,
peering out at life in all its magical abundance.

That's when the rest of me begins to lose its substance
tossed about like flotsam on the surface of the ocean.

The octopus of me lets go of who she really is,
casting off a tentacle in wet despair.

She watches, as it's torn away from her.

And that's when I must gather up the remnants of my second self,
and huddle down beside her.

Together, we wait.

# Danger

We were warned about the jellyfish,
where we paddled, tentatively,
in the shallows, our backs to the sun,
feet braced against the slap of wavelets,
eyes alert for anything globular,
for anything pale, or stringy.

And we were warned about the sinking sand –
sluggish, wet,
sucking at our shoes,
swallowing our shoes.

And the cliffs that might collapse at any moment,
that might crumble to dust
and bury us alive
in a heap of rock and fossils.

They warned us about the danger
of talking to strangers,
of strange men in nightclubs
offering to walk us home.

We were warned to say,
before we set off,
into the mountains,
which path we planned to take,
and exactly when we planned to return.

But nobody warned us about the danger
of sitting, alone, on the sofa.
Or the danger of forgetting to eat,
of not wanting to get up from the sofa.

And nobody warned us of how difficult it can be,
sometimes, just to lace up your trainers,
to open the front door,
to take a deep breath and brace yourself.
To walk outside.

# The clues were all there, strewn out along the shore

If I had stopped to look,
I would have seen the small soft body of a *d*
face down on the sand,

> the flesh of it filled up with brine,
> the ragged tail of it dragging in the damp.

And perhaps I would have found that twisted,
hollow *y*, that piece of driftwood, waving,
arms outstretched, towards the sky.

> I might have laughed, or pulled it down and chopped it
> into bits, or burnt it for a barbecue with friends.

But I would never have spotted that slippery *s*
hidden in the bladderwrack,
flashing in the sun,

> or the sharp *p* of a broken plastic
> bucket, black against the ground.

The pieces that I did find were difficult to understand.
There was the curl of waves across the shore,
the constant *r* of the sea

> and the rough brown *a*
> of a pebble with a hole.

I found cockles and periwinkles,
cracked whelks and razor clams, a starfish
stuck to a rock, the lost home of a hermit crab.

> I found something spiky in a rockpool
> that I couldn't name.

But when I came across an *x* marked out with sticks
I guessed it was the final clue
for a family treasure hunt.

It was only later that I realised
it had been mine to claim.

And there was something about that *i*
stuck on the top of a sandcastle tower, as water lapped
around its buttresses, abandoned to its fate.

But I did not know that then.
It's only now that I can look back and remember

that the delicate shell of an *a*
felt precious, when I picked it up on a solitary ramble,
one February afternoon – the purple sheen of it.

It felt like the beginning of something,
bright, in my hand.

# Diagnosis

After thirty-five years, they hold it out to me –
this offering, this raw
acknowledgement that I am not just
lazy, or clumsy,

that the answers were there all along,
crouching in the shadows,
as I curled my stubborn fingers
around that fat pen, dragging it across the page.

Yes, they say, there was
an explanation
for all those trips and falls,
those bruises, that fear of ice.

Take this new word – *dyspraxia* –
let it illuminate your life.

# Impressions
*after J.M.W. Turner*

                      just      the suggestion

of a painting      or a view

      that isn't there           in the grey illusion

          of a water stain        a woman

      or a ship
                  (its translucent sails unfurled
                     a century ago or more)

      crusted up with tears

that do not fall           or the suggestion of relief

      of not knowing    what comes next

or what this yellow means          or if the sea

      you think you see    is really there

at all

# Understood

They say *yes, you do*
*have dyspraxia*, and this new me
unfolds herself, right there,
in that stuffy office –
her arms and legs unfurl
like a ribbon from a hat,
and we stumble out of there,
together, hand in hand.

Months later,
and she's still here,
curled up with me on the sofa,
head propped up with cushions
as we read another blog post –
helping me to shift each piece
of crumpled memory
into its allotted place.

Slowly, we adjust
our own soft ignorance,
unroll our prejudice
in gentle waves.

# Blue Nude
*after Picasso*

she sits    head bowed    legs curled beneath    he paints
sweeping his brush in slow waves of grey emerging into blue

the light fades from the window    his eyes peer
at her crouched form    low    small    merging with the floor

a faint outline around her skin    a soft halo
he keeps on painting as the light fades    and soon he is painting

in pitch black    he keeps on painting
scratching lines into paint    again and again    spreading

that pale yellow light across her shoulder    filling in
her dark head    the darkness where her head would be

carving her out of the background    bringing her gradually
into the black cave of his studio    his painting

it is so dark he cannot see his hands anymore    she isn't
even there    she never was    and still

he paints    until the town clock strikes three
a cat screeches    he stops    breathes in

deeply    and out again    it is over
he has spilled    the blue of himself    out of himself

he has painted    his blue nude

# Exposure

I walk out, shell-less,
onto the burning shore,
as if

                    nothing can touch me.

As if it doesn't matter
that I trail every hurt behind me in a wet parade
of tears, snot, saliva, flushed and dripping,
heart wide open,
red, against the coarse grey sand.

                              They watch me sideways,
                         from their own thick shells,
                              encased in whorls
                              of stubbornness.

Their silence thickens
and pulsates.

                                        I wince
                                        away.

Their stares bore
into me.

                                   So I wait
              for the

  fury

                    of storm–          lashed

        waves,              thank          ful

                    for the            small

                    relief              of being

        tossed together,
                              in the water.


Briefly, we are
equal,

bedraggled,
sore.




                                        It doesn't last.




As soon as things
are calm again,
they scuttle off to hide,




                                        and all I can see
                                        of them is armour.




18

# The Question

Unfurl it.
> This unasked question.

Release the silken, thick, unbalanced
weight of it:
> the why, the what, the how.

Attach each corner, knot it,
raise it up,
hand over hand over hand.

> Secure it with a twist, to the world,
> then step back. Look up.
> > Let it become its rippled self.

It fights a force that is invisible,
> exhausts itself
> against apparent emptiness,
day after day after day.
> It contorts itself.

You must learn that,
> as it falters
this uninvited question will not fade,
or conjure answers.

> You must walk in the wake of its flight.

# Unremarkable
*after Gwen John*

A woman paints a corner of an attic room, the window closed and
veiled against the heat.

A woman paints a small, secluded corner of herself – an open book
upon the table, open window, open, slanted light. It orients her West,
towards the sun.

A woman paints a corner of her mind, a half-open window, to let the
sunlight in. She paints the scent of a boulangerie, drifting from below.

A woman paints the table in again, removes the book, removes all traces
of herself, begins, again, with spring blossoms and a parasol.

A woman paints because she can, because the universe allows her to.

A woman paints the soft stripe of shadows on the sloping wall, like bars
on a window. She dips her brush, begins again.

A woman is still painting, in a corner of a room, in Paris, in London,
Madrid, in a small unremarkable corner, in a house, a flat, a garden, a
studio.

A woman paints a newer version of herself. This one is polished, yellow,
flat, serene.

A woman paints her way from rue du Cherche-Midi to rue du
Cherche-Midi. But what awaits her there? Another slant of yellow
sunlight in a corner of the room?

A woman paints, a woman writes. A hundred years pass. Another
thirteen years. And here is another corner of another yellow room.

# Exhibits in the Museum of Dyspraxia

An old bruise, dark purple in colour with a hint of yellow, overlaid by a second bruise acquired two days later, smaller, with a touch of green.

Routine, framed and neatly labelled.

A room of unimaginable noise. This is an interactive exhibit. Earplugs provided.

An overflowing hug, in solid gold.

A dropped dinner: smashed plate, spaghetti, bolognaise.

The pulsating aura of a lucid dream.

A lost grip, slipping away.

The pressure of time on the brain.

Spotlights of fascination: the length of a leaf, squawk of a crow, flash of a seagull swooping.

A cushion of air between the body and the mind.

The soft static between memory and recall.

A surge of words that settle on the floor, the chair, the sofa, ruffling their feathers, cooing, waiting.

A duvet cover, forever tangled.

# You See Yourself
*after Elizabeth Siddal*

you see yourself reflected in the glass
a faded figure peering through the mist
an alabaster face is staring back
a pair of lips so red they cannot kiss

a faded figure peering through the mist
you dream of love    a life that could have been
dab lipstick on a pair of thin red lips
add lines to eyes as haunting as they seem

and dream of love    a life that could have been
a flash of light    a movement in the room
his eyes are black    as haunting as they seem
he looks at you    his eyes bore through the gloom

the lamp's too dim    his body fills the room
he dabs some colour on the waiting white
he looks at you    his eyes bore through the gloom
the sun dips down and evening turns to night

a dab of colour on the waiting white
soon he will go    you take a breath    at last
as daylight dims    the evening turns to night
and now he's gone    and all is in the past

so now it's over    take a breath    at last
door slams    alone again    until the next
for now he's gone    and all is in the past
time now to contemplate    to hurt    to rest

door slams                          until the next
          yourself reflected                  glass
time                          to hurt    to rest
a                    face    staring back

# Self-Portrait as Pieces of a Saint
*after Saint Teresa of Ávila*

you may kiss my jaw in Rome
  or grip my finger bones in Ávila

peer through thick museum glass at my shrivelled
  drooping heart and see how they transfigured me

at death into a slice of pious art
  my humble flesh spooned out in prayer

my left arm pinned for you in crystal
  decomposing slowly in its own realm

I am exhumed again
  my skin ripped from its frame

plundered for your touch your taste
  devoured by your curiosity your faith in me

and though you hold the pieces of me in your hands
  I am not here
            I never was

# Missing

You vanish
like a cat, fading from memory, as
I trace the shape of you in the damp night air.

I find your suitcase, empty,
your worn Reeboks on the mat, mud everywhere.
You vanish

again and again, in every April shower,
rain thudding on the roof, dripping on the floor, as
I trace the shape of you in the damp night air,

searching for the clues you might have left,
reaching for the last words you said, but
you vanish

and each time there is a little of you left behind,
in the dent on the wall, the latch you meant to mend, and
I trace the shape of you in the damp night air,

calling you out, peering through the rain,
chanting your name like a prayer, but, again,
you vanish, and
I trace the shape of you in the damp night air.

# Learning to Play

There was an expectation
that every finger would participate,
responding with the same
weight, poise and pressure
as every other finger,
that the eyes would work in sync
to solve this code of dots and lines at pace,
continually working out which line
was which, and if the dots were hovering
above the line, or floating through
the line, or clinging on, beneath.

And was the mind supposed
to focus on the dots, to keep them
still, to stop them sinking?

Sometimes the mind learned
to suspend itself
outside of time,
to let the water take over.

Out would flow
all the wet ripples of the tune,
flashing and rushing,
swift and supple as a stream.

But this trance-like state was loose,
would falter all too soon,
as the mind pushed back,
eager to take over,
and everything would stop.

Sometimes the eyes were too exhausted
to keep the dots from wandering,
and all the dots would jump across the lines,
into the stream, at the same time,
splashing water all over.

Now the fingers rest,
the lines are left behind,
the tongue let loose in verse.
The stream grows, meandering
in twists and turns, from mind
to river mouth, to open sea.

# In the Playground

There was space        (always)        between me and them –

the void opening        as they ran.

I learned to be friends        with the ones who waited.


But there was more I could have known    back then –

that the space between us        was like that between two planets

each spinning on its own axis –

that the ones who waited        would be few


                        that they would not always wait.


But what mattered was not the waiting

no –        what mattered was the spin

of one planet in sync with itself

settled in its own orbit        around a greater sun.

# Balance

She tiptoes out onto the rock and water,
scarf held aloft in a swirl of self-importance
to pose in pure white silk against the backdrop
of children playing in the cascade at Chatsworth.

Their parents yell *It's slippery! Be careful!*
while she pirouettes and stretches out her arms as if to heaven.

Behind her the unlucky children slip,
get their clothes wet,
learn a life-long lesson.

# Growing

Yesterday, a small green bud
sprouted behind my left ear.

Today it began to unfurl,
curling out of itself, reaching

for the light. Tomorrow it will
become a perfect leaf – veins

running down into my core,
spreading its cytoplasm

mucus-like, through blood
and bone. The leaf will grow,

then more leaves will appear,
blooming like tattoos gone wrong

from every pore, stretching out
to catch the rain as I walk,

spread for sunlight, precious
as air, slowing me down,

as I root myself in fertile earth,
in welcome ground. I will grow

into myself, climbing, steady,
grip by grip, leaf by leaf,

dropping my wilted fronds,
head high in my canopy.

# Turning Point

The day I met the horses –
heads hanging, shifting

in our plain suburban driveway.
They shimmered slightly, here

one moment, gone
the next. But they were there

still, when I looked back, when
I look back now, the sheen

of their coats
against the pebbledash.

# Fledge

Stand at the very edge.
Stand at the edge and
look.

Stand at the very
edge and
look down –

down at the whole world spread out beneath:
a mirage of possibility.

Stand there,
flexing your wing –
delicately.

Paper-thin wing,
stretching, and flexing.

Open up your wings as far as they will go –
and back again.

Today
is not the day.
No.

You will go.

Not
today though.

Today is for flexing your wings,
stretching your wings,
opening your wings,

and looking down.

# Two Seconds of Silence

my blank stare     is all you see     where there should be a response
to what you just said     but how could you know     that my mind
is doing back flips     cartwheels     death-defying twists     to get your
words into order     to filter     catch     collate them     to massage their
possibilities into place     test out each scenario     reject it     accept it
again     as I realise you must have said *four* not *floor* while I try my best
to ignore     [yes that]     the white light reflecting off your watch     the
buzz of people coming up the stairs     the thick embrace of woollen
fabric on my arms     the crowd of kids     the screech of tyres     the bra
strap clinging to my skin     the need to pull my own words from the air
[frail     small     pulsating with relief]     as I arrange them here for you
project them out for you     perform this trick for you –

but just as I open my mouth to pour them forth
you say it for me

you assume
that my lax mind is rude
                    and turn away –


But who do you go to when you want to imagine? To forecast
possibilities, scenarios or opportunities? Who helps you when you
need to lift off, away from this tired earth? To fly to the moon and
back again? To turn the sun? To conjure stories from the stars?

Who will take your lines, your rules, your expectations, flip them,
contradict them, wring them out and turn them inside out or upside
down? Who will take your corners and smooth them? Who will tilt the
apex of your spinning world, pause it for a while, bring it to the brink,
and spur you on?

# Dys

I want to dis/
          entangle the sly hiss
of dys, to dis/embowel the fraught
dis/ease of it, as it slips
                    in front, so sure, so certain.

I want to dis/turb its
          dis/avowal, crumple it,
curtail its sudden fist, flung
like an abuser's kiss.

I want to dis/arm the
          beast of it, dis/dain
its dis/approval,
dis/pel its dis/paraging
                    taste, its dull
dis/gust, how it dis/
          figures our praxis,
dis/misses us.

                    I dis/inter dys —

                              its cold corpse

dis/carded

                    on the kitchen floor,

like an old god.

# Absolution

These are the tears that belong to the body of the one who cries them, who loves them from the very start. The one who claims them in their frailty, their gentleness. These are the tears that fall after midnight, the tears that stream down in a hot ungainly gush. Claim the salt of them, as it clings to your wet skin. Claim the silent path of them.

These are the tears that pour, in torrents of hot rain, from headlines on the radio, the tears that burst out from the far-off cry of a child in the street, from the fact that it is too late, after all. Too late to cry for this. These are the empty tears, the ones that flow in currents of despair from a source that gurgles in the soft wet turf of you. The tears that fall in the aftermath of silence.

Claim them, as they drop, one-by-one, into your favourite mug of undrunk tea. Claim the tears that fall for all those years of bubbling frustration. Let them shudder. Let them fling their small bodies like wet daggers at the dry riverbed of everything.

# Mine

I've known you, always,
        in the small pearl of your absence,

                drifting slowly away from me
                across the years.

I've felt your restless waters,
        your crumbling edifice, your waves.

I've seen how dark this cave is,
full of dancing shadows, echoes of echoes.

                There is no avoiding the possibility of you
                    in the ebb and flow of ongoing tides.

I've seen you in the flash of the sun on the water.
I blink, and then you're out of sight.

                I've heard your quiet breath,
                    as you lap against my surface.

Your shore is wide and open, your song a song of life,
your ripples                                       hardly there.

                I've always known how impossible you are.
            A bubble, faint with light. The skin of you so thin.

What would it take to turn you into flesh?

                How can we know what could have been?

# Self-Portrait after a Party
*after Pablo Neruda*

closing the door     at last
            I slip into space

no longer stuck     with legs like awkward trunks     of fragile flesh
      twisting my fake frame     into shape
               holding my     impatient breath

no longer reining in my voice     until it aches
      no longer clinging on to thin remarks
             or stretching out the smile on my face

no longer conscious of each limb
      arranging arms     acceptable and slim
             so that nothing will look     out of place

now

      I can swim     to my own     tune

          shout my own words     out loud     and sigh

now
      I can flow               back and     forth

        become     myself

become     in time     a wisp     of thought

       a slip             of creativity

an animal          of light

# Octopus Mind

You say all that,
about the way your life is faltering,
with such a weight of self-analysis, such questioning,
your eyes avoiding mine.

In the lull afterwards, my octopus mind
reaches out its tentacles
to grasp the core of each word you spoke,

turning them over and over,
tapping them to see what might fall out,
squeezing them to see if they turn sweet or sour.

As the night deepens, each tentacle takes a turn,
latching on, jabbing and prodding,

until each word
is worn down to the bone –

white and shivering,
with scraps of flesh still clinging on.

# I am trying not to write a poem about you

Looking at *Tiger in a Storm*, I imagine
I'm seeing it for the first time,
in a gallery perhaps, hanging high up
on a towering wall.

My overall impression: green,
vegetation, the crashing of the wind,
panic, and there is something there
in all that green: you,

battling your way through undergrowth,
a caveman in your element,
forcing your way inside.

It's too late, you're there now,
stuck between me and the paint,
casting about for a cloak or a hat,
or even a tail, or a pair of tiger eyes,
and there's nothing for it,
you'll have to stay,

so words fill up the space, forming a plot
around the bulk of you,
forging a path for me to join you.

But when I emerge in the green, soaking wet,
peering through sheets of diagonal rain,
all I can see is the tiger.

# Paper Women

I draw them in blue biro on the back of old bills. I give them flat, round faces, arms stuck out either side, a smudge of hair, a too-wide smile. I cut them out and post them to you, one at a time, imagine the look on your face when you slit the envelope and out they drop – these apparitions of myself – one on Monday, another on Thursday, perhaps – more and more of them. Will you recognise me in these paper women? Will you stand them on the kitchen counter, where they can watch you, in silence, as you fill the kettle, as you wonder where they came from, who sent them? How long will you wait, looking into their blue-dot eyes, until you chuck them in the recycling bin, let the lid close with a click, and leave them there, surrounded by old toilet rolls and yoghurt pots?

# Hover

I tried to sleep last summer
but the seagulls were at war    screeching through the dark
and the helicopters hovered    and the pollen drifted in
as I tossed and turned    fighting the pull of you
inside my head    mechanical and raw

each day was worse than the one before    and each look
shot deep or bounced back    and the barbeques were rained off
and no-one could pretend there wasn't something going on
but neither of us said
                                    and now it's summer again
and the day after tomorrow

                                    that's the day            I think

I am determined
                        yes
                                I will        this time
                                                            Yes

# I half-close my eyes

to see a different, more
abstract version of you,

in bold paint,
between impasto layers:

the black of you, the purple,
the rich blue pulse of you,

       the cream and white.

This version of you is still –
this pool of you,

amid the waves of jazz
and chatter.

You don't speak here.
You cannot speak.

       This is the you I savour.

But when the colour fades,
I am left here,

in a cold white corridor,
staring at paint,

wondering

       why a mind would do this
                to itself.

# You have become too much

the cure —

                        to fling my body in       to swim

cold salt water    over skin

                     pummelling each wave

straining every muscle

             in a rhythm you cannot fathom     what humans

have been doing      what horses and bison

    tigers and alligators    have been doing

                 for so long we don't know when it began —

the first swim.

                  I push through    swallowing

gagging on salt    each wave    shocks   cold

    each breath   gasped   held   each stroke propels me

from what was said    and what was not   pulling me

    closer   to the beating   wild

        weeping   heart of me.

# eye / reflections

white claws / hideous
            blasting / at eyes
ark / a vicious light

flick / big / flash / lick / curse / crush / crash jittery
the lank / of green blue throttle / kite
the spike / the golden beast / the flying far / the like
the cairn / the mourn / tornado / super / butterfly
too much / too flit too / slippery / too fight
too strong too / shine too / furtively / too ripe
a cat / a catapult / enrage / the pump of blood
the bark blows pummel / entropy / the blight

must / / some / / times

slowly / / close

these / / too

wide / / eyes

# The Rattle

Spiders are everywhere.
But their trumpets are too long,
and the light bounces in my head, like a wish.

How can I separate the bones
of my frown from the approach
of fresh footsteps in an empty house?

There is a body here, no matter what I do,
no matter how many necklaces I wear,
or how many spiders I catch, and re-position.

There is a false window, a bolt
of barbed red skin, a skirt,
a pulse of conversation framed by snow.

The words drain out of me:
from mice to caviar, from clocks to promises.
Sometimes, the wood can crack.

# Normally

I'm ~~wring~~ writing the ~~wrd~~ word *n-o-r-m-a-l-l-y*, ~~bur~~ but ~~m~~ I'm tired, so ~~aough aluogh~~ although my brain has ~~alry~~ already ~~sipd~~ skipped to the next word, and the word ~~aer~~ after that, my hand is ~~string stinhn~~ struggling to ~~kp~~ keep up, so it ends up ~~inreeeb illlele~~ illegible ~~sble~~ scribble and then I have to go back and ~~reite~~ re-write, but by this ~~pnt~~ point it is so ~~nesss~~ messed up ~~il~~ it makes no ~~ses snes~~ sense, and it is even more ~~ilebe ilebje~~ illegible, so I just ~~es~~ cross it out and re-write the word ~~ain~~ again, above itself. By this time, I've ~~foren ften~~ forgotten what I'm writing about.

# The Lie, Dyspraxia and The Background Hum

When I shake my head, to indicate that
no, I have not caught the words
you threw across to me,
for the third time, it's not
because I'm deaf,
though that's what I say.

And no, unless you actually
raise your voice, or write it down,
or spell the word, or mime it out,
I'll never hear it
above the background hum.

And no, I'm not being rude
when I give up saying *sorry,*
*I didn't quite catch that*
and end up stranded –

             a vacant smile, a halting nod,
             never knowing what you said.

# The Blather

begins, as always,
with a solid silver
line of thought,

twisting, pulling out
towards the light:

                    fine as silk, strong, spooled
from the depths of the mind.

But then, as the mouth begins to open,
it drops
                    away,

leaving nothing –

just a vast hole
of dread, and the hope that words

                    (battered, crawling out
                    on hands and knees)

might bring the silver back again.

A risk, then, yes, but every time,
still, I draw my breath
and take that leap:

I hold on to the silver, try not
to let it slip,
aware that,
if it falls away,

the blather is all I have –

                    just words,

words

          words

# Side Effects of Social Interaction

Five tiny clones of myself
are still sitting inside my mind,
high on adrenaline,
inventing conversation at top speed.

I keep reminding them it's over now.
There's no-one here
to enjoy our pithy comments,
or relish our incredible ideas.

I try not to listen to their forced articulation,
as I change into pyjamas,
close curtains on the world,
lie back on the sofa and drink tea.

Balanced on stiff chairs,
dressed in suits and stretched-out smiles,
arranged around the table of exhaustion,
they keep on rehearsing anyway.

# Self-Portrait with Words and Feathers

The fox appears,
sometimes, in the middle of a sentence –

one moment
I am a safe cage, a netted haven
of preening and cooing, as each thought grooms itself,
fluffing up feathers, shifting on the perch,
hunkering, eyes always alert, and –

                                                                    FOX!

Flaps and fluttering, shricks and nips, and bruises,
a battering of wings, beaks, heads
against the wire, feathers everywhere,

until they settle down again, ruffled, embarrassed
that, after all, there never was a fox, just fear

of what the fox could do, of what might happen
if the cage door opened, if freedom beckoned,

if everyone knew.

# Careful

There's a hawk in my mouth. Every time I open it to speak, she snaps her beak. She is protecting her eggs, hidden among my teeth. Her claws dig into the flesh of my gums. There is a slow, splintering tickle, and I discover a crack forming in one of the eggs, so I take a day off work. I sit there, in my pyjamas, mouth open, in front of the mirror, watching, as a chick begins to emerge. It is pink and scrawny. Damp. There is an unpleasant smell. After a few hours another chick emerges, and then, in the middle of the night, another. They keep me awake with their pathetic mewling. Now I have to be careful not to chew on that side of my mouth. Every few hours the hawk flies off and returns with a mouse or a frog, and I gag on the guts of it. The chicks grow stronger, bigger. My mouth is full of feathers and flapping. I can't think straight. One day, I cough, and out comes a small hawk. I cough again, and again. The hawks fly off. I rinse out my mouth with disinfectant. I'm glad to be rid of them.

# Dyspraxic

Microsoft Word underlines it
                    every single time
in red, as if it isn't real.

Of course not. How could it be?
It represents a              quirkiness, a body
     out of balance          with itself.

It breaks
the rules of social expectation,
        of movement, of        gravity.

It hovers there,
              above that red squiggle,
grinning, defiant.

It dares you to believe        in its existence,
dares you
to be        who you were meant to be.

# Hidden Disability

in a painting        of a tiger
rampaging                through a tropical storm

thrashing terminology
in all directions            knocking

down the definitions
just        out

of sight            bursting wet
through vegetation

and all I can see
is this trail        of leaves            and diagnoses

strewn all over            with no real path
to show where            or how I fit

or how I can begin to split
his striped shape

to paint it on myself
or roar it        to the world

*after 'Painting of a Tiger in a Tropical Storm' by Henri Rousseau*

# Post-Diagnosis

The trunk of me has settled –

now that it knows
where to root itself,

now that the rain makes sense,
                               each drop of it
                               expected now,

now that the snow –

the weight of it,
the sudden
shock of it,

                 makes sense.

And now the storms come gradually,

like old friends,

and the creep of wondering       has dissipated          into clouds,

and the rocks
          still make me
stumble,

but now it is       ok because

                 they have names.

# The ghost of hard work will be there, always

hovering above the sofa,
whispering in your ear,

blowing gently in your face,
sending you notification after notification.

The ghost of hard work
will force you to listen

to people on the radio talking about debt
and increasing levels of unemployment.

The ghost of hard work
will hide in the creases of your wallet,

in between the pixels of your online bank statement,
curling around the edge of each direct debit,

grinning at you from behind each
frivolous transaction.

Sometimes you will manage to ignore it,
to get your head down,

get on with what you have to do,
but it will come back in the middle of the night,

floating above your pillow,
turning itself over and over,

over and over and over.

# Nine Brains at Midnight

The first brain wallows in the ache. It rolls the body over and over.
Adds a diagnosis of a Terrible Illness or two to the ongoing list.

The second brain is trying to block out That Evil Noise from next
door's flat that sounds like bullets on a wheelie bin.

The third brain is planning a Really Fantastic Seminar that it will
deliver in a few months' time, working out the sequence of the tasks,
and pushing them unceremoniously, one by one, into the expanding
memory bank.

The fourth brain grins as it recalls That Really Funny Thing from
yesterday.

The fifth brain is trying to remember the name of the tree we met
beneath during lockdown, in the rain.

The sixth brain is singing.

The seventh brain is composing a poem about a person who lies awake
at midnight, composing a poem.

The eighth brain is scripting a conversation it will never have.

And the ninth brain is wishing that the other eight brains would Just
Shut Up and let it dream.

# Sleep Paralysis

Your mind stumbles out of bed, leaving the shell of your body behind, and everything is black or gold or white or red. You lie there, mute, as you fumble your way from one room to the next, wondering why you cannot seem to move your legs. And you know you are awake, and yet you cannot be awake. And your head is a rock, and your body is dead. Then somebody moves, in the bed beside you. Sitting there, in the bed beside you. Lying there, on the bed, beside you. Hot breath, right there, beside you. Try to scream, but you can't move your mouth, and you know you are awake, and yet you cannot be awake, and your head is a rock, and your body is dead. Breath on your face, and the face comes close, you cannot defend yourself, their body next to yours. So you try to scream, but you can't move your mouth, and you know you are awake, but you cannot be awake, and your head is a rock, and your body is dead, and you try to scream, but you cannot move, and then you wake.

And the day is a wrench, with an ongoing ache. And your eyes want to close, but you must stay awake. And the world is a cave in which you dread. And the day is a wrench, the mind bled dry. And you'll never know what, and you'll never know why.

# The Test

I went to be tested. They sent me into a booth, told me to stick this swab into the back of my throat, and then up my nose. To twist and twist. I thought it would make my nose bleed, but it didn't. Instead, what came out was a rush of tiny corpses. Each one looked like a miniature version of me. Each one was so small I could have squashed it flat between my finger and thumb. They piled up on the table, fell to the floor, tumbling over one another. I stood up, legs shaking, and my nose was still spewing corpses. Nobody seemed to notice, so I just tiptoed through, trying not to step on any of them, and fled, holding my nose to stop the flow. It was only when I got outside that I realised it was too late. All of my old, dead selves had spilled out of me.

# Our Bodies

Our bodies are more than bodies now.
They sing out breath and vulnerability and hope.
We can't stop looking at each other's faces –

lips all different shapes, all shades and textures,
our smiles tender and lopsided, our noses.
These bodies are more than bodies now.

They are giants of humanity in skin,
with all our hurt, our fear, our joy inside us.
We can't stop looking at each other's faces:

stretched and beautiful like ballet dancers,
raw and clear and open as the sky. Yes,
our bodies are more than bodies now.

They hold themselves out, sculpted, full,
proclaiming life, proclaiming who we are.
We can't stop looking at each other's faces.

We fill this room with physicality and soul,
with the unsaid countless absences among us,
in bodies that are more than bodies now.
We can't stop looking at each other's faces.

# Familiar, Divergent

It stretches [blank] across the mind,     hides itself
    in gaps       or hesitations

appearing in the flicker
        of eyes      half-closing.

It pulls the body down
            in all directions
      snaps itself at [edges]

lining up the muscles
      for collision with chairs   doorways      [questions].


It drags the feet           fumbles around fingers
      digs in piles of discarded wonderings

      retreats
beneath the surface, to a safe space.


It simmers there for decades
                  [undetected].

The scent of it.
The weight of it.

           And when the spell breaks –

it surfaces:
wave after wave of clear, uninhibited release.

# Sorry

I'm late, in Swansea, signing in, and *sorry*,
says the lady, as we enter,
*sorry*, again, as she signs her name,
*sorry*, dropping the pen on the floor,
*no, it's ok, sorry, I didn't realise… I didn't mean…*
as we both walk off down the hall,
and then I'm me again, though late,
yes, and stressed, leading the workshop for them,
hearing *sorry* whispered every now and then,
an echo of it served up with a laugh each time,
and in the end I just have to give in and let her be sorry –
this lady who has been sorry all her life,
sorry that she doesn't understand, or cannot spell,
sorry that she needs a little bit of extra help,
sorry that the numbers won't add up no matter what she does,
sorry that she takes up space in the room that could
have been given to somebody else.

And I'm thinking of her a year later, now that I know.
And what, really, is the difference between the two of us?
And I'm thinking back to the sign-in sheet in Swansea that I scribbled on,
because my hand could not manipulate the pen,
and how I didn't even think that that was odd,
at the time, I just thought that I had to pretend,
pretend that everything was normal,
and there she was, not pretending, but saying sorry,
and now it's time to say to it to myself –
*I'm sorry*, and move on.

# On Waking

A barn owl lands,
silently, in the kernel
of my mind.

I watch as she swallows
her prey in one gulp,
ruffles her soft white feathers.

She swivels her head
without a sound,
listening for something.

It is at times like this
that I have learned to pause,
to lie there and feel

the lifting of her wings,
the grip of her talons,
waiting for the moment

when she departs.
And I am left to wonder
where she came from,

where she goes,
holding my mind out
to catch

a single feather,
drifting
in the dark.

# Self-Portrait as a Neurodivergent Tree

The trunk of me lumbers
through neurotypical streets: flat
      blocks of concrete, tarmac, brick.

I dip and sway around each corner,
      squeeze through rigid
            expectations, balance
myself across their rules,           teetering
      on the edge
         of their constrictions.

My roots long for soft,
           fertile ground,
for the unencumbered
         embrace of earth and fellow trees,
      their branches open, swaying
in gentle, empathetic welcome,
      where notions flutter, floating
                off
      without complaint, where each
tree thrives in its own
      anomalous, divergent space,
         sending out its shoots in all directions.

People point, whisper,
      stare at my unruly branches,
my uneven pace,
         afraid they
      might catch something of my
         tree-like nature,
            drop
a thought or two, be forced
to flex
      their rigid
      perceptions.

We trees stand proud,
> hold out our canopy
>> adorned
in white and green –
> the mantle of our creativity
bursting into bloom.

# Acknowledgments

Thank you to the editors of the following publications where some of these poems, or earlier versions of them, first appeared: *Anthropocene, Poetry Wales, One Hand Clapping, Visual Verse, Raceme, The Open Mouse, Ink Sweat and Tears, Confluence* and the *Marble* broadsheet.

Thanks to the organisers and judges of the following competitions, where some of these poems were placed. 'You See Yourself' won the Pre-Raphaelite Society Poetry Competition in 2021, and was nominated for the Forward Prize. 'Understood' was runner up in the Bangor Poetry Competition, 2021. 'Missing' and 'You See Yourself' were shortlisted for the Bridport Prize, in 2019 and 2020. 'Exhibits in the Museum of Dyspraxia' was highly commended in the Liverpool Poetry Prize, 2021. 'Hidden Disability' was highly commended in the DAC Creative Word Award in 2022. 'Diagnosis' and 'You have become too much' (under a different title) were commended in the Ware Poets Open Competition in 2021. 'Self-Portrait after a Party' was commended in the Cheltenham Poetry Festival Competition, 2021. 'Unremarkable' was shortlisted for the Gloucestershire Poetry Society Open Competition in 2021. 'Self-Portrait as a Neurodivergent Tree' was longlisted for the Mslexia Poetry Competition in 2021.

Many thanks to all those fellow poets who have encouraged and supported me over the years, in particular: Christina Thatcher, Katherine Stansfield, Jonathan Edwards, Philip Gross, Abeer Ameer, Amy Wack, Helen McSherry, and Heather Trickey. Thanks also to Rhian Edwards and Zoe Brigley, and the Seren team. And to fellow members of Roath Writers, who have been so supportive.

Thanks also to my PhD supervisors Damian Walford Davies and Richard Marggraf Turley for their ongoing support and encouragement, and to my tutors and fellow students at Cardiff University, Manchester Metropolitan University, and Aberystwyth University.

Thanks to the South West and Wales Doctoral Training Partnership for funding my PhD, allowing me more time to develop my writing.

Much gratitude to friends and family, without whom I would not have written this book.